The Prestige Se

Bedwas & Machen

Michael Yelton

© 2010 Venture Publications Ltd

ISBN 1905304404
ISBN13 9781905304400

CONTENTS

Title Page
Albion, HAX 340, had a much more rounded body than the first, also built by Welsh Metal Industries. It was caught in Caerphilly in 1949.

Acknowledgements
All black and white photographs in this book are from the camera or collection of Roy Marshall to whom we record our thanks. We are grateful to David and Mary Shaw for their meticulous proof-reading of the text.

Michael Yelton
November 2010

INTRODUCTION

The Bedwas and Machen UDC transport undertaking in South Wales was well-known among bus enthusiasts because it was for some years the smallest municipal operator in the country: later that distinction was held by Colwyn Bay in North Wales, which ran only a promenade service for a period of time and later by Hartlepool (as opposed to West Hartlepool) Corporation, which ran only four vehicles on a joint service with its neighbour. However, the operations of Bedwas after the Second World War were more complicated than is sometimes supposed and there were many features of interest in the fleet.

Bedwas and Machen (more properly Upper Machen) are two villages on the main road between the substantial town and transport junction of Caerphilly, which historically was in Glamorganshire, and the very large town, now city, of Newport, which was in Monmouthshire. Until 1912 the Bedwas and Machen area was part of the St. Mellons Rural District, but in that year a new Urban District was formed, which consisted of the two named villages and the intermediate settlement of Trethomas (sometimes, particularly at that time, written as Tre Thomas). Even Lower Machen, a separate and more rural village further towards Newport, was excluded from the new administrative unit.

The new Urban District was in the county of Monmouthshire and thus technically not part of Wales until 1974. Its southern boundary was the Rhymney River, which divided Monmouthshire from Glamorgan, and ran very near the settlements. To the north west, the Urban District included a considerable area of open fields and hills, and also the village of Maes-y-Cwmmer, which was strategically placed on the main road between Blackwood and Ystrad Mynach and was connected to the rest of the area only by a narrow road from Bedwas along the side of the hill. The population of the UD in 1911 was 4,936 but by 1971, shortly before its abolition, this had increased to 12,540. The acreage was originally 6,520 but after an exchange with the neighbouring Mynyddislwyn UD in 1935 this was reduced to 6,179.

Although neither of these villages could properly be described as belonging to the classic South Wales valley model, as they were not anything like as stratified in construction, they were originally very dependent on coal mining, as of course were most of the other local areas.

In the nineteenth century, Machen was the larger village, and Trethomas did not exist. There was coal mining in Machen but this ceased with the closure of the Old Pit in about 1920 and the focus of industrial development moved to Bedwas. As the nineteenth century moved on, a number of small drift mines were opened in Bedwas, but it was the sinking of the very large Navigation Colliery in the village (or more exactly in Trethomas) in 1909, which was to produce by far the largest local employer. It was completed in 1913 at the very height of production in the South Wales coalfield. The pit, later known simply as Bedwas Colliery, was closed after the miners' strike in 1985, allegedly because of geological difficulties.

Those difficulties had plagued the colliery throughout its life, and resulted in serious labour problems which included a two months' closure in 1928 and riots in Bedwas in 1933 after the employers had introduced non-union labour to the pit. In 1939 there were 1,850 men working in the colliery and that year the record of 675,000 tons was raised, much of it steam coal for ships: hence the name given to the pit.

In the post-Second World War period the area expanded quite rapidly, with new housing being erected to cater for those who commuted to Cardiff or Newport. Both Bedwas and Caerphilly grew outwards so that there was only a very small gap between the two. The most significant single development, however, was the decision in the 1960s to construct a comparatively large housing estate at Graig-y-Rhacca, just to the east of Trethomas and behind the main road from Caerphilly to Newport, which brought with it an obvious need for transport facilities.

The Bedwas area was served by several of the many railways which were constructed in South Wales primarily to carry the coal to the docks at Cardiff and at Newport. However, the main line through the area, the Brecon & Merthyr Railway, although connecting Newport with Machen (where there was an engine shed) and Bedwas, did not enable residents of Bedwas to go to Caerphilly. The line turned north to Dowlais and eventually to Brecon: there was another station at Maes-y-Cwmmer, which provided the only direct connection by public transport between the southern and northern parts of the Urban District. A branch from Machen, which featured separate up and down lines with their own unidirectional halts, did run to Caerphilly, but that did not pass through Bedwas. In any event the railways in the area were primarily for the carriage of coal rather than of passengers.

It is sometimes thought that Urban Districts were in a special or disadvantaged position so far as the operation of transport undertakings is concerned, but this is quite wrong. Under the system of Local Government introduced in 1894 there was a strict hierarchy of authorities. County Boroughs, which were given powers equivalent to County Councils, were at the top: they were generally towns with a population of 100,000 or more, although the status was not generally removed if the town declined in size, as for example did Merthyr Tydfil. The next category comprised Boroughs, generally consisting of substantial towns with a population of up to 100,000, and then beneath them were Rural and Urban Districts. Although in the post-Second World War period there were relatively few Urban District Councils which operated transport undertakings, there was no legal obstacle to their doing so, and it may be that their relatively small size and the financial risks involved put off many. In South Wales the Urban Districts, both adjoining Bedwas and Machen, of Caerphilly and Gellygaer (later Gelligaer) in Glamorganshire both operated buses. In addition the West Monmouthshire Omnibus Board, another neighbouring operator, although a separate legal entity, was formed by the Bedwellty and Mynyddislwyn UDCs.

Elsewhere, Aberdare and Pontypridd in South Wales, Llandudno in North Wales and Ramsbottom and West Bridgford in England also ran buses and Eston UDC had a one third share in the Tees-Side Railless Traction Board. None of these save Aberdare and Pontypridd had operated trams or trolleybuses and most of the remainder were relatively late starters in the provision of transport facilities. However, earlier there had been a number of UDCs who had operated trams but did not then run buses, the most obvious of which were those in the Metropolitan area which were taken over by London Transport on its formation in 1933, such as Barking Town, Leyton and Walthamstow.

What made Bedwas and Machen unusual was that the Urban District did not, as in for example Pontypridd, centre around a moderately sized town, but rather covered what can only described as villages. Also ,it had a much smaller population than Gelligaer, which included more settlements, although none of them individually was very large. There was a strong sentiment in the area that municipal transport would not only reflect local pride but also prevent profits going to companies based elsewhere and the powerful tradition of the Labour Party in South Wales was a further factor which encouraged such developments. It is ironic that the Rhondda Borough Council, which was in a hot bed of Socialist and even Communist support, did not run its own services, but rather had them provided by the arch pro-capitalist BET through the Rhondda Transport Company.

Under the Local Government Act 1972, which took effect on 1 April 1974, the Urban District of Bedwas and Machen ceased to exist. It was also transferred from Gwent, the new name for what had been Monmouthshire, to the new county of Mid-Glamorgan, together with Rhymney and with part of Bedwellty Urban Districts, and incorporated into the new Rhymney Valley District Council, which also included the former Caerphilly and most of the former Gelligaer Urban Districts. The effect on the transport undertaking is set out later.

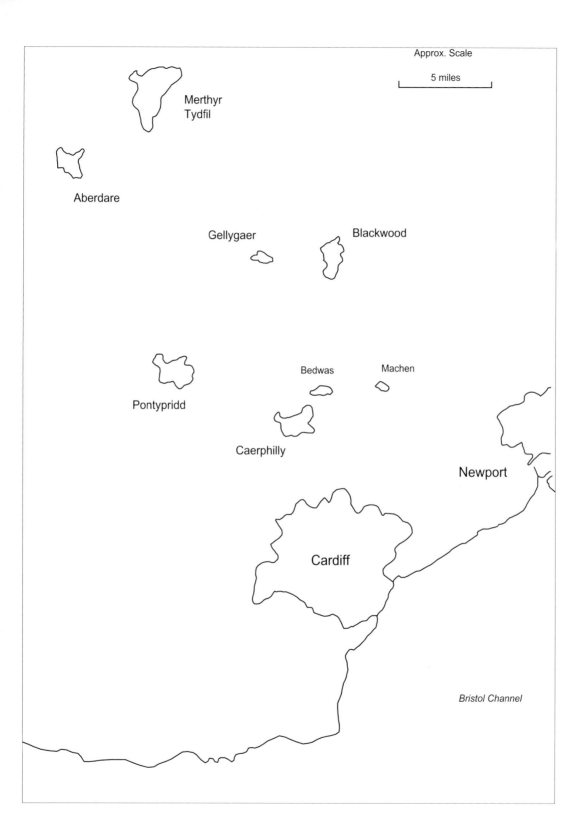

Approx. Scale

5 miles

Merthyr
Tydfil

Aberdare

Gellygaer

Blackwood

Pontypridd

Bedwas

Machen

Caerphilly

Newport

Cardiff

Bristol Channel

One of the first vehicles run by the Council was this Straker-Squire, which arrived in 1922.

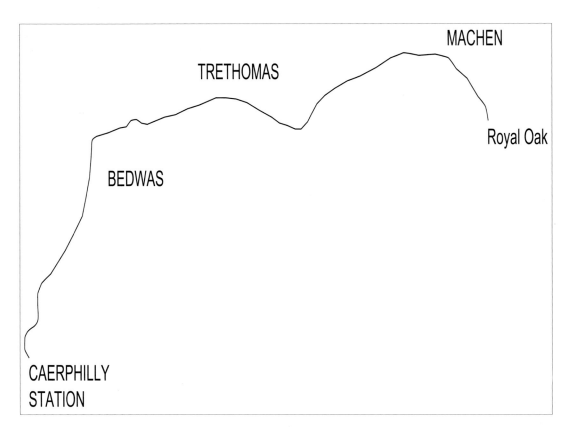

Bedwas and Machen route, pre-war.

HISTORY OF THE UNDERTAKING, 1922-45

The authority was granted powers to operate buses under the Bedwas and Machen Urban District Council Act of 1917.

The Act was one of three granting powers to run buses to Urban Districts in South Wales all of which received the Royal Assent on 2 August 1917. The others were in respect of Caerphilly, which closely concerned Bedwas and Machen, and Ebbw Vale, which did not, and where in any event the powers were never taken up.

The Bedwas Act was extremely restrictive in its terms. By section 5 the Council was authorised to provide buses and to run them only (a) anywhere within their area and (b), with the consent of Caerphilly, along a carefully specified route from Bedwas Bridge (the boundary) to Caerphilly Railway Station. They were given the power to spend initial amounts of up to £3,000 on buses and up to £800 on property and facilities. It is interesting that the Colliery Company was one of the supporters of the bill: it was originally opposed by the South Wales Transport Company (SWT), which had been running from Caerphilly, albeit not to Bedwas: it later retreated to Swansea after the grant of powers to the local authorities in the Rhymney Valley.

The Caerphilly Act was similarly very limited in the powers it conferred. The Council was able to run from Caerphilly to (a) Penyrheol and Sengenydd and (b) Bedwas Bridge. It could also run from Bedwas Bridge to Trethomas, but only with the consent of Bedwas and Machen UDC. There was provision also for running anywhere else within its area if authorised by a subsequent provisional order, one of which was granted by a further Act in 1921.

Both the Acts of Parliament clearly envisaged that the two adjoining Councils would cooperate together. In section 14 of the Bedwas Act it was given the power to enter into running agreements with other bodies and by section 15 to enter into a joint committee with Caerphilly. The latter's Act gave corresponding powers and it appears that a joint transport committee was envisaged as likely to come into existence almost immediately.

However, although the powers were given to Bedwas in 1917, services were not actually introduced until 12 January 1922. Caerphilly, on the other hand,

began running to Nelson via Ystrad Mynach in April 1920 and shortly thereafter to Sengenydd, a route which had been abandoned by SWT.

Bedwas and Machen set up a Legal, Parliamentary and Motor Omnibus Committee of the Council, which met frequently both before and after operations actually began. After the Second World War it simply became the Motor Omnibus Committee.

The minutes of the committee, which in earlier years were written out in hand by a clerk in the Council offices and in later years were typed, show clearly the realities of small town life in South Wales. Everyone knew everyone else at a time when jobs outside of the pit were highly valued and the committee took upon itself the responsibility of deciding who should be given permanent or even temporary employment with the Council. Initially, there was no separate transport department, because of the small size of the operation, and the buses, and indeed the civic ambulance, which was the subject of much discussion in the committee, were in 1924 made part of the domain of the newly appointed Engineer and Surveyor to the Council, HFH Gibson, who was also termed Omnibus Manager.

On 5 September 1919 it was resolved to purchase two buses but shortly thereafter it was suggested that there should be a joint meeting with Caerphilly, which had indicated its own desire to run to Bedwas in accordance with its statutory powers. On 19 September 1919 it was suggested that there be four buses a day from Caerphilly to Machen, and that the main service be to Trethomas, hourly until 1pm then every 45 minutes until 5pm, and then every 30 minutes. The apparently odd system of increasing frequencies as the day went on was typical of industrial areas of South Wales. It was also suggested that private operators be licensed to run until the Council was ready to start its own operations, which seems a somewhat foolish proposition as competition would have been difficult to dislodge.

The matter then seems to have gone to sleep for some time, perhaps because of the economic problems which affected many areas after the Armistice. However, on 26 November 1920 it was resolved to buy three Fords at £500 each. Less than a month later, on 20 December 1920, this decision was apparently abandoned, as it was resolved instead to purchase two second-hand

AEC double-deckers and to ask Caerphilly UDC for provision to operate into their area.

There was clearly a considerable degree of antagonism and mutual suspicion between the two Councils, with Bedwas considering that its larger neighbour, across the county boundary, was unreliable and domineering. However, on 16 March 1921 Caerphilly "eventually", as the minutes record, agreed to Bedwas' request to run in their area.

Almost a year had gone by since the resolutions to purchase vehicles and no buses had arrived. However, on 30 September 1921 a new motion was agreed, to the effect that two Straker-Squire single-deckers be purchased at what appears to be the high price for the time of £1,535 each. It is characteristic of the way in which the business of the Council was then conducted that on 7 October 1921, a week after the taking of an apparently clear decision, it was resolved that a visit should be made to the Commercial Motor Show at Olympia with a view to inspecting not only Straker-Squire products, but also those of AEC, Dennis, Thornycroft and Leyland. However, when the order was actually placed it remained with Straker-Squire.

Things were moving forward at last. On 25 November 1921 there was an important meeting of the committee at which it was decided that the two vehicles on order would be licensed with effect from 1 January 1922 and that three drivers and three conductors would be taken on. It was agreed that the service would run from Caerphilly to Trethomas (thus with no extension at that stage to Machen) and that the terminus at the outer end of the route would be the corner of Newport Road and Glyn Gwyn Street, with no service on Sundays. The livery of the vehicles is discussed in the next section, but it was agreed on this occasion that the lower half be 'peacock blue' and the upper half white. Advertising was carried from an early stage.

One of the problems with the way in which the committee went about its work was that it concentrated too much on the trivial without regard to the wider picture, a common criticism of small local authorities. Thus, on 14 December 1921, it was agreed after extensive discussion that there be free travel for policemen in uniform, but at that time no concluded agreement had been reached with Caerphilly about their involvement in the running of the proposed service, which was clearly a much more important, indeed fundamental, matter. It was not until 6 January 1922 that a meeting was had with Caerphilly for the granting of formal permission and there was only then talk about a joint timetable and a joint committee, as had been foreshadowed in the 1917 statutes.

The next few years were to see wrangling and posturing between the two adjacent local authorities and at one stage even legal proceedings. At an adjourned meeting on 11 January 1922 Caerphilly made it clear that they wanted to run on alternate weeks, which was a wholly unsuitable arrangement for Bedwas as it would have meant that their vehicles were not in use for half the year. It was finally agreed, in order that the service could begin the next day, that in the following week, commencing 16 January 1922, Bedwas should run until 3.30pm and thereafter the service should be jointly run, the next week Caerphilly would run until 3.30pm and thereafter there be joint running and that from 30 January 1922 there should be joint running all day. The mid-afternoon watershed, which was to be of considerable significance over the next few years, thus originated as a compromise to end temporarily the unseemly squabbling between the local authorities.

After that last minute agreement, operations finally commenced on 12 January 1922 using the two new Straker-Squires, which had rear entrance bodies and seated 32: they were registered AX 3860 and 3861.

A small depot, which lasted for many years, was established on the Newport Road in Bedwas, next to the Council's offices, past which the service ran.

The agreement between the two authorities was, however, only intended as a short term compromise. It was renewed on similar terms with effect from 8 February 1922 but thereafter there was a hardening of attitudes on the part of Caerphilly and on 17 March 1922 they threatened to refuse permission to Bedwas to run into their area unless they could run the morning service on alternate weeks: they then said that if agreement could not be reached, they would run only so far as the bridge on the boundary and would not continue to Trethomas. However, on 16 June 1922 they suggested joint running (which is what Bedwas had always advocated) but by this time the smaller local authority was full of pique and on 30 June 1922 they refused the offer.

In the first year of operation 195,000 passengers were said to have been carried by Bedwas, which demonstrated the need for the service whatever the wranglings behind the scenes.

In early 1923 Caerphilly brought proceedings in the Chancery Division of the High Court claiming an injunction to restrain Bedwas and Machen from running in their area without permission, and this seems to have brought matters to a head. On 18 May 1923 a meeting of a joint committee of both councils was finally held and it was agreed that for an initial period of three months Bedwas would run the whole service until 3pm and thereafter it should be run jointly. It also appears that prior to this meeting Bedwas had run a limited service from Caerphilly beyond Trethomas and on to Machen, terminating in the Chatham area to the east of the village, but these then ceased for a time. Caerphilly had, of course, no statutory power to run beyond Trethomas and so could not participate in that service.

On 8 June 1923 Bedwas' own committee discussed the purchase of a third bus to run as a feeder from Machen and also to provide workmen's services to the Colliery: on 6 July 1923 the purchase of a Karrier for £921 was approved, and in September of that year a forward entrance vehicle of that model arrived and was thereafter used for early one man operation, largely as a feeder from Machen to Trethomas.

It appears that the feeder was initially successful, as on 27 December 1923 it was agreed that on Fridays and Saturdays it should be replaced by the extension of alternate Bedwas journeys from Caerphilly right through to Machen. However, as soon thereafter as 10 January 1924 it was resolved to discontinue the service to Machen save on Fridays and Saturdays, and then on 7 March 1924 to lay on late night services all the way through. Workmen's buses between Machen and Navigation Colliery continued. Predictably, Caerphilly complained that the extra Machen journeys dislocated the joint running which had been agreed.

Prior to this time, there was no through service between Newport and Caerphilly, although in 1923 T Beavis of Danygraig House, Risca, who traded as the Danygraig Bus Service, began running from Newport to Machen (Post Office), which is in the centre of the village. Beavis had started his bus operations in 1922. In 1924 Thomas Davies of Abertridwr wished to commence a

through Sengenydd-Caerphilly-Bedwas-Machen-Newport service but, united for once by common cause, both councils refused him permission to run through their areas.

In early 1924 it became clear that a fourth vehicle was required, as the two Straker-Squires needed overhaul. The Council vacillated between employing a mechanic and asking an outside firm, Frank Gaccon & Co. of Cardiff, to assist. On 25 March 1924 it was agreed to purchase another Straker-Squire at a cost of £1,200: significantly, the price had fallen from that of the first two, reflecting trade conditions. On 13 June 1924 it was agreed that instead of employing an in-house mechanic the two original vehicles would be overhauled by the manufacturers at a cost of £177.10s.

On the same day the long running problems between the two local authorities were finally compromised. It was agreed at a meeting of the joint committee that Bedwas would run the service until mid-afternoon and thereafter it would be joint, but that Bedwas would only use two vehicles on the service. On 3 October 1924 Bedwas agreed at a further meeting of the joint committee that they would cease one man operation on the Friday and Saturday service to Machen, but shortly afterwards resolved not to abandon that service. They also suggested that there be a Sunday service on the main route and in late 1924 agreement was reached on a new timetable: shortly afterwards Sunday running was agreed. Peace at last reigned between the two Councils.

However, the economic conditions meant that the fleet did not much expand: in late 1925 Karrier agreed to supply a new bus for £1,685, a six wheeler with capacity for 39, which was not to be exceeded until double-deckers were introduced, and to take back in part exchange the one man bus, allowing £685 for it: this transaction took place in 1926.

During the 1920s there was great hardship in the South Wales coalfield because of the collapse in the price obtainable for its products and the consequent industrial unrest, including later the very long miners' strike which partly coincided in time with the General Strike of 1926. As early as 30 January 1923 it was agreed, after considerable debate, to reduce the wages of the road staff by a penny farthing an hour. Leisure travel was not a high priority.

Although in early 1926 the workmen's buses were said to be overcrowded, thereafter there was a rapid decline in receipts and in the year ending 31 March 1927 there was a deficit on operations. Later that year AX 3861, the second of the original Straker-Squires, was reported to have been partially dismantled and would require six months off the road. On 11 November 1927 it was agreed that in the light of the then declining traffic the frequency of the service would be cut from every 20 to every 30 minutes on Mondays to Thursdays and from every 15 to every 10 on Fridays and Saturdays.

In 1927 there were also two competing proposals in the air, either of which would have seen the end of independent operation by the Council. The first, which was to be floated on a number of occasions later, was for the creation of a Rhymney Valley Board comprising Bedwas, Caerphilly, Gelligaer and West Mon, an objective which was not to be accomplished until the local government reorganisation in 1974. Agreement could not be reached at that time. The second was for the sale of the undertaking to TR Jenkins, a local entrepreneur and politician who at one time ran Western Services Ltd., as a front man for the Watts interests who in due course gathered together their operations as Red & White. That again did not proceed.

The late 1920s also saw the railway companies deciding to take a much more active role in the provision of road passenger transport. The most vigorous in that regard was the Great Western Railway, which had commenced running services in many places within its sphere even though the legality of such enterprises was somewhat doubtful. Following the enactment of the Great Western Railway (Road Transport) Act 1928, the position was made much clearer and the capacity of the GWR to run bus services was undoubted. However, that Act, by section 3, precluded the Railway Company from running in competition with a bus service run by a local authority save with the consent of that authority, but permitted it to run from outside into or through the local authority area provided the same passenger was not picked up and set down within that area. By section 11 the Railway Company was also given the power to make agreements with local authorities for joint running.

The GWR was anxious to expand in South Wales, and in due course it adopted the policy which the other railway companies also took up, of investing in road transport by using associated companies in which they had a shareholding. In this area, the railway interests were invested in what became Western Welsh, which merged the railway operations with some previously carried out by South Wales Commercial Motors Ltd.: the "Western" in the title, like "Southern" in Southern Vectis, represented the connection with the Railway Company rather than having any geographical connotation. Even prior to their Act passing, the GWR had been negotiating between Caerphilly and Bedwas and Machen with a view to taking over the service to Trethomas and starting a through service to Newport, which had originally been floated by Caerphilly.

In a further statute, the Caerphilly UDC Act 1928, that authority was given the power to operate through services to both Cardiff and Newport, but only in conjunction with the transport departments of those municipalities respectively. Caerphilly then began running to Cardiff in what was to become the southern portion of the through service to Markham (later Tredegar) after West Mon joined them shortly thereafter, but they never came to an agreement with Newport.

Beavis' service between Newport and Machen continued at this time to run hourly. In 1928 his business was offered for sale, and Newport Corporation agreed to buy it in April of that year, but the obduracy of Magor and St. Mellons RDC, through part of the territory of which the route to Machen ran, caused the deal to fall through. The eventual purchaser was Mr. J Williams of the Allied Building Corporation, who used some services as an ancillary to the construction of new estates, but in June 1932 he sold the bus business to a local consortium which ran it through a limited company, Danygraig Omnibus Services Ltd., running from East Usk Road, Newport. In 1933 that company was running from Newport to Machen, to St. Mellons, and to Risca, with some journeys to Pontymister.

Newport's failure to acquire the route to Machen meant that it never became involved with services along the Rhymney Valley and meant also that Caerphilly could not itself proceed with a through service. Caerphilly were by this time also not averse to giving up their share of the

Trethomas service, on which they had expended so much time and effort.

Times were indeed hard. On 26 March 1929 Bedwas discussed competing offers to purchase the undertaking from Jenkins (again) and Lewis & James of Newbridge, a business which had been running services since 1919 but in 1925 had sold out to the National Electric Construction Company, which already ran the tramways in the Borough of Rhondda. The approaches were rejected only on the casting vote of the chairman, and when the matter resurfaced on the agenda only a month later, on 22 April 1929, it was narrowly agreed in principle to sell the concern to Jenkins, but in fact that proposal never proceeded.

By late 1929 it was agreed that at least one of the Straker-Squires should be sold and noted that the Karrier had broken down. Shortly thereafter it was confined to workmen's services.

By 1930 Western Welsh were operating an isolated route between Ystrad Mynach and Bargoed, in the area of Gelligaer UDC, which was shortly to become important in the development of bus services further down the Rhymney Valley.

The other major non-municipal transport undertaking in South Wales was the then privately owned Red & White group, based in Chepstow, but it then had no involvement in services in and around Caerphilly, but, as in other areas, was anxious to expand.

There was a general scramble around the country to establish new routes before the Road Traffic Act 1930 came into effect on 1 April 1931, and Western Welsh, as successors to the GWR, continued to negotiate with the councils of Newport, Bedwas and Caerphilly for a through service taking in those three places. On 3 March 1930 a deputation from Bedwas met representatives of Newport Corporation with a view to asking for cooperation in allowing the UDC to run through from Caerphilly. Newport confirmed at that meeting that they had agreed in principle with Western Welsh for the introduction of a long overdue through service.

Caerphilly UDC had by this time put themselves out of the picture so far as a route to Newport was concerned, and had agreed in principle with Western Welsh to hand over their interest in the Trethomas route.

On 31 October 1930 Bedwas and Machen agreed with Western Welsh that they would operate jointly on the Caerphilly-Newport service, with the municipality having a 25% share. However, Bedwas could not put that agreement into force at that time because they had no specific statutory power to operate into Newport under their own Act: after the coming into effect of the Road Traffic Act 1930, which was not to happen until 1 April 1931, they could so run provided that the consent of the Traffic Commissioners was given under section 101 of the Act. Existing municipal operators were given by the Act a general power to run within their own areas, but could only run outside them with the consent of the Commissioners. On 30 December 1930 it was agreed to make application under section 101 to run to Newport.

Probably in 1930, and certainly by 9 February 1931, which was an important cut-off date under the new Act, Western Welsh had begun an hourly service between Newport (High Street Station) and Caerphilly, which is described in the timetable as being a "coordinated service with Bedwas and Machen UDC". At the same time, they ran the journeys from Caerphilly to Trethomas which had previously been the responsibility of Caerphilly, and thus after mid-afternoon they ran the service jointly with Bedwas. Thereafter, Caerphilly never did run into Bedwas on stage services, although they did run workers' services as we shall see later.

There was another curious interlude: in September 1930 one Edgar James Davies, who was associated with Red & White, also began running on the Newport-Caerphilly service and borrowed three vehicles from his backers, but the route only ran for about seven months before it was abandoned.

Bedwas had, therefore, eventually declined to be absorbed by Western Welsh or any other outside operator. There was great pressure not to do so as the political culture of the area was to foster municipal trading and prevent profits being given to outside shareholders: this was a potent factor in all South Wales local authority transport.

On 4 May 1931, in one of the early decisions under the Road Traffic Act 1930, Bedwas were granted permission by the Commissioners to continue running from Caerphilly to Machen and it is clear that at some point prior to that some journeys on the service were extended to Machen (Royal Oak), which is on the Newport side of the village just beyond the previous Chatham terminus, and thus there was a slightly greater overlap between that route and that of Danygraig. The independent tried to extend further across Machen in the Caerphilly direction, to the White Hart, but never got permission to do so.

By this time economic conditions were improving considerably and the monthly number of passengers, which had dropped to 18,000 in 1928, had risen to 30,000.

Bedwas, having decided to remain independent, was anxious to expand its field of operation in accordance with its agreement with Western Welsh and on 27 April 1931 further agreed with them that the service between Caerphilly and Newport should be every 30 minutes with every fourth bus being run by the municipality. On 25 June 1931 the Traffic Commissioners held a public meeting at Newport to consider the Council's application under section 101 to run outside its area to Newport. They refused it, for reasons which are not now clear, but which bemused the local authority. No appeal was mounted, but they wrote unsuccessfully to the Minister asking for clarification of the use of the powers under section 101. They also recriminated against Western Welsh, whom they thought had done them down at the hearing by unexpectedly announcing that they would grant protection to the Danygraig Motors service.

The move to expand thus hit the rocks of statutory regulation and for the next twenty years the operation remained restricted in its geographical scope.

Western Welsh then applied to the Traffic Commissioners for a half hourly service from Newport to Bargoed via Machen, Bedwas, Caerphilly and Ystrad Mynach, joining together the two routes they were already operating with a new section between Caerphilly and Ystrad Mynach. The application was granted, but as Caerphilly UDC already ran over this portion of route on their service to Nelson, they were granted protection. The frequency was, however, only to be hourly, as opposed to every half an hour. The route ran north west from Newport and then changed direction at Caerphilly, so that it ran almost due north through to Bargoed, providing many useful connections, and began in 1932.

The "joint service" between Caerphilly and Trethomas continued as before save that Western Welsh took the place of Caerphilly in the post-

3.30 period, when running was every 15 minutes: Bedwas had the mornings to themselves and also ran through to Machen on Friday and Saturday. One provision in the Road Traffic Act which was of benefit to them was section 105, which allowed a local authority undertaking to run services in conjunction with other local authorities or with any other operator, without specific statutory powers.

By 1930 the pioneering Straker-Squires were reaching the end of their useful lives, and contact was made with dealers called Child & Pullen in Ipswich, who agreed to take all three for £50 each and also to supply a second-hand NS (known as Daimler although possibly technically an AEC or ADC), from London General, which duly arrived thereafter. At about the same time two small Albions which had originally been operated by the Port Glasgow Motor Company were purchased from the manufacturers acting as dealers and a Gilford was acquired from United Automobile. The Albions were used for one man operation on workmen's services and in late 1932 the Traffic Commissioners insisted that the capacity be reduced from 25 to 20 in accordance with the provisions of the 1930 Act. By that time one of them was, in any event, too run down to be of further use and it was returned to Albion.·

Earlier that year it had been resolved to purchase one new and one reconditioned vehicle. The new vehicle appeared in the spring in the form of an Albion PW65 (costing £729) with Park Royal rear-entrance body (costing £395). Against it Albion took the Karrier. The search for a suitable second-hand vehicle proved fruitless and it was suggested that the NS be refurbished at a cost of only £25, although it was then disposed of the following year. Early the next year a second-hand Albion, EU 4577, owned by Atlas Garages, was suggested but its purchase fell through and instead another new Albion with Park Royal body was purchased in March 1933.

The arrangements for the joint service did not persist in the immediate post-Road Traffic Act form for very long. A Western Welsh timetable for 1934 shows that they then only operated extra journeys between Caerphilly and Trethomas about hourly on Fridays and Saturdays from 3.15pm.

By 3 May 1937, when Bedwas issued a new timetable card, they had, however, themselves considerably improved their service so that it ran approximately hourly between Caerphilly and

Machen, reversing in Royal Oak Lane, with extras to Trethomas. By the outbreak of the Second World War, the position had stabilised along those lines, although by then their extra journeys to Trethomas ran only on Fridays and Saturdays. It also appears that most of the workmen's services had been given up and certainly one RG Heath of 4, Green Row, Machen, is stated to have run buses from that village to the pit at Bedwas.

By then operations were run by an all-Albion fleet. The two new vehicles bought in 1932 and 1933 proved successful and so, in 1936, an example of the later PW69 model was acquired in lieu of the survivor of the small Albions, which was said to have been out of action for about 18 months. The Gilford was disposed of in 1935 and so the second-hand vehicles disappeared and the fleet was steady at three buses for some time.

It was thus a very small but no doubt valued enterprise at that time, with just the one relatively short route. The only expansion proposed was that in 1936 Bedwas and Machen suggested to the West Mon Board that there should be a joint service from Bedwas, along Pandy Road out of the village, and than along the narrow old road to Maes-y-Cwmmer. This did not attract any interest from the Board: nor did a rather more sensible, although still financially very risky, suggestion in 1938 that a joint service along a similar route but right through to Blackwood should be commenced.

In July 1935 Western Welsh absorbed Danygraig, although they continued to use that trading name for some time thereafter, eventually ceasing to do so in October 1940. In their 1939 timetable they showed hourly services from Newport (High Street Station) to Bargoed alternating with further hourly journeys between Newport (Mill Street) and Machen (Post Office) which were still described as being run by Danygraig. In a relic of the previous arrangements between Bedwas and Caerphilly, Western Welsh said that they did not ply for local traffic between Caerphilly and Trethomas before 3.30pm: thus the local traffic was at least partially protected in favour of Bedwas and Machen.

The War, of course, imposed very considerable strains on the transport arrangements of nearly all operators and it seems that Western Welsh ceased what had become its vestigial service on the short workings from Caerphilly to Machen. On 20 January 1942 it was decided to curtail some of the Machen journeys at the White Hart and on 8 December of that year it was resolved that all services finish at 9pm to save mileage and fuel. The restrictions on Western Welsh competing between Caerphilly and Trethomas disappeared with the advent of the war.

Despite the national conditions, the mutual antagonism between Bedwas and Caerphilly continued. In June 1941 Caerphilly asked whether a workmen's service they were running from the Treforest Industrial Estate to Trethomas via Caerphilly could then pick up passengers on what would otherwise have been a dead journey back to the depot: this apparently reasonable request received a short and negative reply.

In late 1942 the Council was told that it was to be granted a licence to acquire a Bedford OWB, the only single-decker then being produced. They replied, perhaps not fully understanding the way in which matters had developed, that what they really wanted was another Albion, but no vehicles of that marque were being constructed at that time for bus use.

The historic hostility between the two adjoining Councils was about to change in the face of a genuine emergency. Early in the morning of 5 February 1943 there was a disastrous fire at the Bedwas depot: the entire three vehicle fleet was completely destroyed, an unparalleled event in the annals of municipal bus operation. The manager's car and a lorry were other casualties. Of the three Albions which were burned out, one was in any event without an engine, which was away being overhauled. This demonstrates clearly exactly what a small-scale operation was then being run.

Although relations between Caerphilly and Bedwas had been so frosty, in the immediate aftermath of the conflagration Caerphilly lent vehicles to Bedwas to allow the service to continue. In fact at an emergency meeting of the transport committee later the same day, it was noted that every single scheduled journey had been run, including the 4.45 am workmen's special. However, when later that year Caerphilly asked for support for a revived Rhymney Valley Transport Bill they received a disparaging answer.

After a relatively short time, the first of four Bedford OWB buses arrived, which then formed the fleet for the next few years. By an extraordinary coincidence, in the following year Caerphilly in its turn had a fire at its depot and on this occasion Bedwas reciprocated the assistance which had been given.

At the end of the War, therefore, Bedwas had probably the most modern rolling stock of any municipal operator, albeit it was all to utility standard and comprised entirely of 32 seaters. There was considerable overcrowding and by 1945 40,000 passengers a month were being carried, by far the highest ever figure.

In 1944 the Council took delivery of its fourth OWB, EWO 924, seen on the Pandy Road service on 16 July 1949. The bonnet side had gone missing by this time.

As this photograph taken on the same day in Caerphilly shows, the off side bonnet side had also gone missing.

HISTORY OF THE UNDERTAKING, 1945-74

At the end of the War, the Council was still running on only the one route together with some workers' services. Western Welsh confirmed at the end of the hostilities that they did not propose to reintroduce the pre-war locals to Trethomas, so Bedwas was left in sole control of the short route.

The UDC timetable issued on 15 April 1946 showed little change from that which had been in force in 1939. However, in South Wales, as in all parts of the country, there was a very great rise in travel for leisure purposes and locally there was particular pressure on public transport because so few people had access to cars. In addition, mining was locally enjoying something of a final flowering of prosperity under the new National Coal Board, and Bedwas was beginning to grow with new houses being constructed. On 12 February 1946 the Transport Committee considered that serious thought should be given to the acquisition of double-deckers, because of the overcrowding. The other small neighbouring municipalities, Caerphilly and Gelligaer, had both acquired double-deckers for the first time during the war, as had the West Mon Board.

In late 1946 it was proposed that a stage service be run to Pandy Road, Bedwas, along which the abortive proposed route to Maes-y-Cwmmer would have run. It was also proposed to Western Welsh that a joint half hourly service be introduced between Caerphilly and Newport, in order to fulfil the idea which had been blocked by the Traffic Commissioners in 1931.

It was September 1947 when the Commissioners gave permission for the route from Caerphilly to Pandy Road, where it terminated at the junction with Pandy Mawr Road on the outskirts of the built up area. Pandy Road is narrow and lined with typical terraced houses. The service was initially to run in the afternoons only and in any event could not be introduced immediately as there was no spare driver available and no vehicle for the route. On 1 October 1947 representatives of the Council inspected two second-hand vehicles being sold by Praills (Newport) Ltd. at Hereford. One was HPL 337, a 1939 Dennis Lancet II with Dennis centre entrance coach body previously owned by Yellow Bus Service of Stoughton near Guildford, which was viewed with suspicion on the grounds that it

was too new a bus to be sold if it were satisfactory, although in fact the real reason may have been that smaller vehicles capable of one man operation were required for the service on which it had normally run: the other was ANT 244, a 1938 Bedford from MH Elcock of Ironbridge, which did not appear very attractive. Eventually, it was decided to buy another Bedford OWB which was purchased from Arlington Motors in Cardiff and had previously been owned by Ralphs of Abertillery. It arrived in November 1947 and enabled the Pandy Road service to commence.

In the meantime, the substantial increase in passengers and the small capacities of the Bedfords which were in the fleet led the Council to the significant decision to acquire four double-deckers. At that time it was still extremely difficult to obtain new buses, especially for a small organisation with very limited purchasing power, and so a two pronged plan was arrived at, although both initiatives were to lead to delay and difficulty.

A short term solution was decided upon in the acquisition of two 1930 Leyland Titans with lowbridge Leyland bodies, which had been run in the traditionally very well maintained Wigan Corporation fleet. They were purchased in November 1947 from Watts (Factors), dealers in Lydney, who formed part of the Red & White group. However, although diesel engines had been fitted by Wigan, the vehicles required overhaul by Watts, which took a very long time. The first, EK 7913, arrived in September 1948: the second, EK 7912, did not arrive until late in 1949, as it was found that it needed rebuilding, which was done by Modern Vehicle Constructors of Caerphilly.

While these were awaited, Bedwas pressed on with the other limb of its scheme, the purchase of its first new double-deckers, which were on Albion CX19 chassis such as were more usually found in South Wales with Red & White but conformed to their own pre-war predilection for that manufacturer. They were bodied locally by Welsh Metal Industries (WMI) of Caerphilly, to the factory of which Bedwas actually ran works services. They were one of the many small bodybuilders which attempted to meet the enormous demand of the time, but the company's move into bus bodies from aero engineering was, however, unlike some of the other newcomers, a complete disaster, and had even begun with an argument with the local UDC over refurbishment work, which resulted in their being

The first new double-decker purchased by the undertaking was GWO 482, which arrived in early 1948 with an angular body by Welsh Metal Industries. It was seen at Caerphilly by Roy Marshall on his 1949 visit.

GWO 482 was substantially rebuilt to remedy the deficiencies in the bodywork. Its livery was also modified and it lost the white top deck windows. It is seen here in Machen on an unknown date.

denied any further work from Caerphilly. They then rapidly acquired a very poor reputation for reliability, as vehicles took a very long time being bodied even after the chassis had arrived from the makers: that in itself was subject to substantial delay at a time of unprecedented demand.

The company had, as with others moving in the same direction, been involved in aircraft production during the War, and they attempted to use the same techniques in manufacturing bus bodies. No timber at all was used, and very little steel: the bodies were constructed of aluminium alloys, and the initial design (which was used on the first Bedwas vehicle) was extremely angular in appearance, looking rather like the most austere utilities of a few years before. This form of body was subject to extensive adverse comments from customers, and was modified to a more rounded version, as used on the second Bedwas bus. Neither was an aesthetic or practical success, not least because, as with some other WMI bodies of the time, the windows were mounted by putty and progress along the road was marked by extraordinary rattling and vibration. However, after radical rebuilding and the introduction of more conventional rubber mountings for the windows, the Albions did have full lives with Bedwas.

Not surprisingly, Welsh Metal Industries ceased supplying to the domestic market as early as 1949, although they did provide bodies on some small Austins for export thereafter. Only about 33 double and 4 single deck bodies were built new for British operators.

These general problems manifested themselves with the two Bedwas buses. Mr. Gibson, the long serving engineer to the Council, seems to have had some input into the construction of the bodies, and before the deficiencies became apparent the authority wished to give him a bonus payment. The chassis of the first vehicle, GWO 482, was delivered to WMI in February 1947 but did not enter service with the Council until February 1948. By October of that year it was returned for repairs and as early as October 1952 it was rebuilt by Romilly Motors of Cardiff and the windows mounted in the more conventional rubber. It was later recorded that even after that its single-skin roof led to condensation dripping.

The second vehicle was not sent to WMI until June 1948 and was received by the Council, more reasonably, in October of that year, and was not rebuilt with rubber mounted windows until June 1954: the work in this case was carried out by Caerphilly Council.

The eventual arrival of the double-deckers eased the overcrowding and a regular system of duplicates to Trethomas was run, some of which turned via Navigation Street, Standard Street and Lower Glyn Gwyn Street and were shown separately in the timetable. The garage could not initially take the new vehicles and land at the back was cleared for them but it was decided that this yard could not be covered.

There were other signs of expansion. In February 1948 Bedwas began participating in a works service run by Caerphilly from there to the Northern Aluminium Company (later Alcan) at Rogerstone: this again led to incessant wrangling between the two authorities and claims that the service was uneconomic. Bedwas was continuing to expand, and from September 1949 permission was given for another new service, again initially running afternoons only, from Caerphilly into the village and then along Church Street, the spine of the settlement, and Rectory Road, to terminate at Brynfedw Avenue, in a new area of housing. It saved the residents walking down to the main road and to Bedwas Square. Most journeys came from Caerphilly after arriving there from Pandy Road.

The character of the fleet changed radically from this time to cope with the new demands being made upon it. After the introduction of the double-deckers, thereafter nearly all new vehicles were of that layout until the arrival in the later years of the Council's life of high capacity underfloor engined single-deckers: the exception to this were two half cab single-deckers which were placed in service in 1951 and were used to run most of the journeys on the Pandy Road service as well as other work. They arrived just as a very steep decline in the numbers of new half cab single-deckers was beginning, but were extremely handsome vehicles bodied, again locally, but this time by Bruce of Cardiff using East Lancs frames, which produced a much better result than had been achieved by WMI on the Albions. The other quotations received were for Albion Valiant CX39 chassis, also to have Bruce bodies, for Fodens either engined by themselves or by Gardner, to carry bodywork by ACB of Sunderland, and for Crossleys with the manufacturers' own bodies.

In 1954 HAX 340 was refitted with conventional rubber mounted windows and is seen here in 1958 in its later state, in Caerphilly.

The Bruce bodies on the AECs had full width canopies and rear entrances and in many ways represented the culmination of an era of design which was soon to end. The vehicles served Bedwas for many years despite the fact that they were obsolete almost as soon as they arrived. The appearance of the two buses was the more commendable because Bruce built only 13 new single-deckers in three batches, of which this was one: most of their work was on double-deckers and the majority of those was for Cardiff Corporation. The Bedwas orders were amongst the last completed by the company and a further order for a body on a Leyland PS2 for Caerphilly UDC was not fulfilled and was transferred to Massey.

In 1950 Mr. Foster finally retired and it was decided that the increased need for administration should be met by the appointment of a dedicated Transport Manager for the undertaking. The post was given to Godfrey A Coleman, who had previously worked in the Council's rating department: he must not be confused with the gentleman of the same surname who dedicated his entire working life to the West Mon Board.

The new transport manager found there was an immediate need for economy after the spending to renew the fleet, which had not been entirely successful. The two former Wigan double-deckers were not in service for long: as early as July 1950 EK 7913 needed an extensive rebuild as the crankcase had broken, but when it was found that extensive work was required to the bodywork it was sold to Morlais Motors of Merthyr. The other lasted until 1951 and was sold to a showman. The Albions needed, and were eventually given, radical rebuilds as described.

Another expression of the need to raise revenue was the provision on the two new single-deckers of large wooden advertisement boards above the side windows: these were part of a new contract signed by the local authority at that time with agents called Griffiths & Millington in Cardiff.

In 1952 another new double-decker arrived in the form of an AEC Regent III with Northern Counties body similar to three supplied the previous year to Aberdare. Its highbridge configuration remained unique in the Bedwas fleet and certainly the committee noted that the cost of a highbridge body was no greater than that of a lowbridge. What seems clear is that the lowbridge configuration, which was not then a necessary requirement for any of the routes run, made use in the wider area more flexible because of the large number of low railway bridges in South Wales.

The first of the two AEC Regals supplied in 1951 is shown in Caerphilly on 26 September 1952. Number 6, is fitted with the distinctive side advertisement boards.

On the same occasion, a nearside view of JWO 354 shows that two different beers were being advertised.

In June 1953 Mr. Coleman gave notice that he was moving on. His replacement, EV Thomas, was to be in charge at an important time for the undertaking.

There is no doubt that 1954 was a crucial year for Bedwas and Machen. In most places, the high water mark for numbers of passengers carried was at or around that time, but the particular factors surrounding the area meant that in the case of this undertaking, this did not occur until 1960, when a million was reached for the year. What was particularly impressive was that, having reached a million passengers a year in 1960, Bedwas was able to maintain a steady level of about 900,000 from 1964 to 1973, at a time when other more prestigious operators were suffering from very serious declines in traffic.

In 1954, however, there was a complete reshaping of the still modest operations.

At that time, Western Welsh were still operating the Newport-Machen-Bedwas-Caerphilly-Ystrad Mynach-Bargoed service in the same way as it had run when they took over the Danygraig company. Thus there was an hourly service right through commencing at Newport (High Street Station), which was interspersed with the former Danygraig service, also hourly, but leaving from Newport (Caxton Place), as did all the routes taken over from that company, and running only as far as Machen (Post Office). Route numbers had still not been introduced on what was a complicated network. In the 1954 timetable there was a rather odd note which indicated that Bedwas and

Machen might in due course make representations about the renewal of the pre-war joint service to Trethomas.

Bedwas and Machen and Western Welsh, however, came to an agreement in June 1954 that the two short overlapping services should cease and that instead there should be an hourly service from Newport to Caerphilly, jointly operated by the two undertakings, with the existing hourly Newport-Bargoed service continuing, which was to be run by Western Welsh alone. In order that this agreement could be put into effect, the Council, of course, still needed permission from the Traffic Commissioners under section 101 of the Road Traffic Act 1930, which had been refused in 1931.

A public sitting of the South Wales Commissioners was arranged for 15 September 1954 to consider the variation application on the licences and also the application for consent for external running under section 101. These were granted and the new arrangements were put into effect from December 1954. This was clearly a sensible solution from the point of view of the travelling public, and it was also extremely significant from the perspective of the Council, because it raised the profile of their operations very considerably. It meant that their vehicles were seen in the major conurbation of Newport rather than only on the short routes from Caerphilly.

As well as this significant reorganisation of the old-established route, there were further applications in that year. The Council surrendered

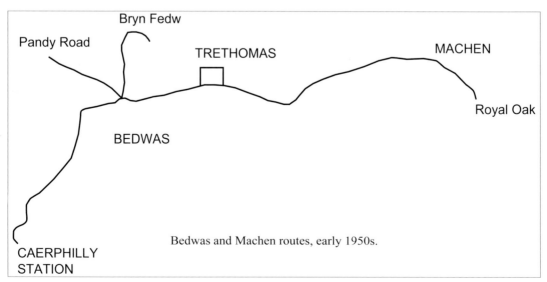

Bedwas and Machen routes, early 1950s.

On 5 May 1953 the second Regal, number 7 in the old livery but still advertising beer, was seen on the Brynfedw service.

John Gillham visited the old garage on 15 April 1960 and saw JWO 355, the second Regal poking out.

The only highbridge vehicle operated was AEC Regent III built with a series for Aberdare by Northern Counties. Number 8 is seen here in Caerphilly on 28 May 1956.

By 1960 at the latest white upper window surrounds had been applied. No.8 is seen at the back of the depot in Bedwas.

the licences for all short running journeys to Trethomas on the main road service and for all journeys to Brynfedw Avenue via Rectory Road. In lieu, a new service to Trethomas via Llanfabon (the designation carried on the blinds) was applied for, which became known in due course as the back road run. This was again from Caerphilly and it followed the existing Brynfedw line up Church Street, but then went more directly via the estate area, passing Brynfedw Avenue where the other service had turned round, and then through Llanfabon and very near the Navigation Colliery to Trethomas (Standard Street) where it terminated at the corner of Glyn Gwyn Street, very near to the main road through the village along which the original route ran, but on the loop previously used by duplicates. A short-term licence, later confirmed, was granted for this with effect from 9 August 1954.

In early 1955 the Council was able to issue a new reorganised timetable schedule, in which there was regular operation on each of the three routes. The main road service between Caerphilly and Newport ran hourly, although, of course, there was joint operation with Western Welsh on it. The Caerphilly to Pandy Road service ran two hourly, and Caerphilly to Trethomas via Llanfabon hourly. The system as then working was obviously very different from that which had been in place even as lately as the end of the War and far more extensive.

Van Parish Council also asked at this time whether some Pandy Road services could be diverted from the main road between Caerphilly and Bedwas to run via an area known as Forset, but this was not thought appropriate because of the state of the roads. What did happen, and it is not clear when, was the extension of some journeys to the Miners' Hospital at Caerphilly at visiting times.

In 1956 passenger services on the railway between Newport and Caerphilly via Machen ceased, which may have boosted the main road route marginally.

In the same year the first of a series of five AEC Regent V vehicles arrived, delivery of which was spread between then and 1964. The first was by far the most unusual in that it had an exposed radiator, rare on the Regent V, and bodywork by Longwell Green of Bristol, a company used by other local municipalities: the others had more conventional enclosed "new look" fronts and bodywork by Massey of Wigan, who had a particular niche in the municipal market. The Longwell Green body was a one off design by the bodybuilder of lightweight construction, using a great deal of aluminium. It arrived on 1 November 1956, being ordered partly at least because the Albions needed recertification, and before the end of that month the bodybuilders were asked to carry out further work on it as there was "a drumming noise from the roof".

The Llanfabon service became something of a money-spinner even in the form in which it was introduced. A Sunday service was introduced with effect from 24 June 1956 and then from 1959 the basic frequency became 30 instead of 60 minutes. Because of the way in which it had developed, the Council had managed to secure this line without any joint operation with either Western Welsh or Caerphilly and it was an economical service to operate because the terminus at Trethomas was only a short distance from the garage, and the end-to-end running time was only 15 minutes. In early 1957 the works service to Welsh Metal Industries in Caerphilly ceased, although the licence was not finally surrendered until 1965.

After the reorganisation of 1954, passenger numbers increased and so did the size of the staff. By 1957 the undertaking still did not require any rate support and there were seven drivers and seven conductors employed.

One source of endless discussions in the committee was the need for a new garage. In 1955 there were moves to relocate either to an old dairy site on the main road nearby or to land which now forms part of the Pant Glas industrial site behind The Avenue at Trethomas. The latter proposal won the day, but nothing was ever done to take it forward. In July 1956 the Ministry of Transport refused permission to borrow £5,465 which was required for the construction of the new building, and then after a minute in January 1957 to the effect that a new garage was a "real necessity" which should be built "as soon as possible", it was discovered that the proposed site had quicksand on it and was wholly unsuitable. On 29 May 1958 the topic resurfaced and it was said that the roof of the existing garage was in a "deplorable condition". Various suggestions were made as to an alternative location, such as The Bryn, Trethomas, and an allotment site in Pandy Road (which would have been very difficult because of the narrow approaches). By this time it was thought that a new

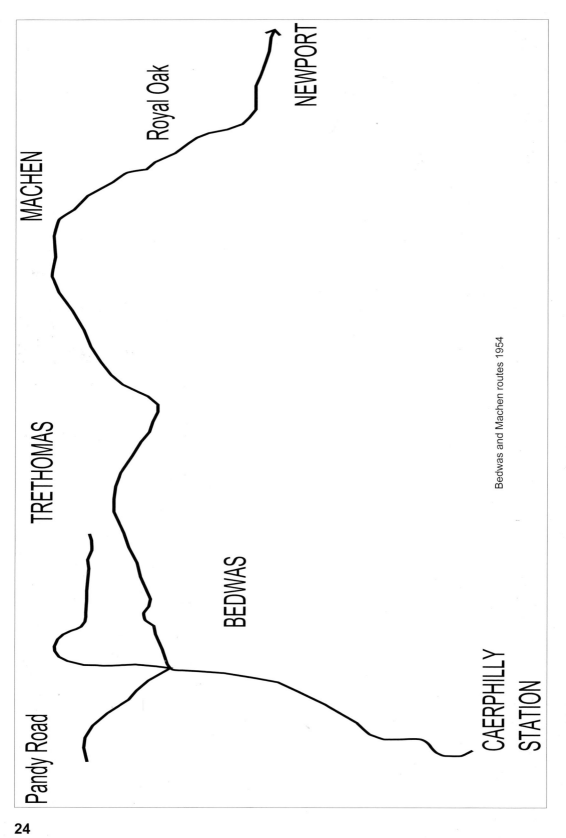

Pandy Road

TRETHOMAS

MACHEN

Royal Oak

NEWPORT

BEDWAS

CAERPHILLY STATION

Bedwas and Machen routes 1954

In 1956 the first of a number of lowbridge AEC Regent V models was taken into stock. PWO 783 had an exposed radiator and bodywork by Longwell Green. It was seen on 17 July 1961 emerging from the old garage.

The next Regent V, number 10, had Massey bodywork and a concealed radiator. It was photographed on the Trethomas service in Caerphilly on 30 September 1967.

garage would cost up to £30,000, although it would be much less if the Council's own workmen built it using direct labour.

Finally, in January 1959, it was resolved to clear the site of the old garage and to build on the opposite side of Newport Road, Bedwas, next to the imposing Workmen's Hall. Even then the financial implications had to be worked out: in September 1960 it appeared that the Council could borrow £18,000 of the then estimated cost of £27,000 for the new garage and in 1961 work began. The old garage was initially handed over to the municipal surveyor but has since been demolished: the new garage, on a section of road now bypassed by the main road, is still in existence although no longer used by the local authority. It was larger and better equipped than its predecessor but was destined to have a short life in its original guise.

One of the evident problems with an undertaking of this small size was the constant inclination of the committee to micromanage instead of leaving decisions to the Omnibus Manager to deal with. Thus, hours were spent on discussing alleged misdemeanours by road staff, the most prominent of which was a conductor called WC Timothy, who seems to have been a trial for many years. Initially, he worked part time and complained about the irregularity of work affecting his unemployment benefit; later he was reprimanded for leaving his bus vacant at Machen while he went to watch a boxing match. He was then hauled before the committee again after an umbrella which had been left on a bus was recognized by the loser in the hands of the conductor's wife. The committee appear to have been satisfied by the convoluted and unlikely explanation which he came up with.

While so much time was expended on these matters, and on the then revolutionary decision in 1955 to employ a woman driver, which was not in fact taken up, important matters such as reorganising the route pattern or the purchase of a new vehicle costing a considerable amount were reached very quickly.

When Western Welsh finally introduced route numbers, the through route to Bargoed became 506 and the joint short workings to Caerphilly were 507. Rather curiously, Bedwas on occasion issued timetables only for the 507, ignoring the journeys on the 506 in respect of which they had no direct interest. In 1959 a bus station was opened in Dock Street, Newport, and all the external routes ran into it instead of into the scattered terminal points around the centre of the town and in that year a contract service was begun to Bedwellty Grammar School, well outside the immediate area.

The route pattern established in 1954 continued for a number of years. In 1957 the first of the AEC Regent V double-deckers arrived with Massey bodies and enclosed radiators. In January 1958 the manager delivered a detailed report on the state of the vehicles, in which he said that the two Albions, which by then were running only a small weekly mileage, were reasonably sound: however, by September of that year the committee was told that the first of the pair was in a hopeless condition and that another new AEC should be purchased, which manifested itself as the second of the Massey bodied vehicles, 11 (UWO 698). In February 1961 the second Albion was considered to be beyond useful repair, and at the end of that year it too was replaced by an AEC, which took the number 5 (422 CAX).

At that time, the financial state of the undertaking remained very good, with a healthy profit of about 10% on turnover that would have been the envy of most other transport operators. A policy decision was taken on 25 July 1961 that a new vehicle would be purchased every other year, and that any other surpluses would be used to repay the costs of the new garage, which at that time was almost ready.

The policy for fleet renewal so formulated was never rigidly applied, because fairly soon economic conditions began changing for the worse. However, in 1964 the highbridge AEC was withdrawn after a relatively short life and was replaced by the last of the Massey bodied Regent V vehicles, 8 (BWO 585B). There were still some members if the Council who wanted to see a direct service between Bedwas and Maes-y-Cwmmer, as had been proposed in the past, and in late 1962 the manager was asked to report on a suggestion that the Newport-Caerphilly service be extended to Blackwood, so that it only required one bus journey to reach one part of the Council's area from the other, albeit not by a very straight route. The manager delivered an impressively tactful reply, pointing out the many difficulties which an application so to run would have faced, apart from the perceived lack of traffic. The idea was floated again the following year and then

The third Regent V, the second with Massey bodywork, number 11, arrived in 1959. On 1 August 1968 it was climbing out of Caerphilly.

Massey were selected again to body the next Regent V, numbered 5, which arrived in 1961. It was pictured in Bedwas on 15 May 1964 bound for Newport.

finally disappeared. A more sensible suggestion, which was put into action, was the diversion of a morning service to serve Newport railway station en route to the town centre.

The financial position deteriorated with some rapidity as more local residents acquired their own transport, a development which took place later here than in many areas. By mid 1965 Bedwas and Machen was definitely feeling the pinch, and in early 1966 it was resolved to cease operations on the Pandy Road service, which had limited traffic potential as so few side roads had been constructed off it, and to cut down the Colliery services. Consideration was also given to diverting the Trethomas via Llanfabon route to the more direct Hillside Terrace instead of penetrating the increasing congested narrow roads of the Bryntirion estate, but no decision was taken to that effect. The general situation was not assisted by labour problems, which became acute in late 1967.

One possible solution to the problems was the resurrection of the idea of a transport board for the whole Rhymney Valley, which was seen as a means of cutting costs. This was raised again in March 1966 and the following month it was at first resolved to have joint discussions with Caerphilly, but then decided that since changes in local government were inevitable there was no point in initiating reconstruction at that time. Caerphilly for its part thought that all four authorities concerned, Bedwas, Caerphilly and West Mon, had to meet before anything of substance would result, and that did not happen. The Board in particular was strongly opposed to any such negotiations which would have compromised its independence.

It was not until 1967 that a number of significant changes were made, and even then the initiative came from outside the Council. By the late 1960s both Western Welsh and Red & White were suffering from loss of passengers, which was accentuated in both their cases because their networks overlapped in so many areas, meaning that there was gross over-capitalisation of facilities such as garages and the like. In 1967 there was a major reorganisation which provided for joint running between the two companies on nearly all the services in the Valleys, and led to the closure of some depots.

It was agreed then that Bedwas should participate in the through service from Newport to Bargoed as well as the short workings to Caerphilly, presumably for easier scheduling, and Red & White also began operating jointly on the service, which acquired the number 150. Bedwas convinced itself that there would be financial benefits from running on the extended route and had resolved to buy a new vehicle only if the revised arrangements were approved.

The timetable for 4 June 1967 identified the journeys actually run by Bedwas as being four to Bargoed and four to Caerphilly from Newport: in other words they ran along the whole route about every four hours. They did not run it on Sundays at all.

That change coincided with the beginning of the building of the new estate at Graig-y-Rhacca which has been mentioned in the introduction. A short distance beyond the Trethomas terminus what became a substantial settlement was erected around a circular pattern which the buses traversed in an anti-clockwise direction: the main road was named Addison Way and there were some cul de sacs leading off it, but the direction taken by the buses meant that passengers did not generally have to cross the road to catch them.

In October 1967 about 6 journeys a day were extended there from Trethomas, but by 20 July 1968 there was an hourly service to Graig-y-Rhacca and only on Saturdays were additional short journeys to the former terminus retained. The half hourly service instituted in 1959 had been something of an over-provision before the estate was built, but by January 1973 the extended route was running hourly on Monday to Fridays and half hourly on Saturdays, and in October 1973 more journeys were put on. A workers' service was also begun in 1971 from Graig-y-Rhacca to the Pant Glas Industrial Estate at Bedwas: in the same year it was resolved to cease the Colliery services unless the National Coal Board would subsidise them (which they refused to do) and also to give up the Rogerstone service, about which there had been so much disagreement. At that time there were other workers' services to the Virginia Factory and the Pontygwindy Estate at Caerphilly and school services to Bedwas itself, Trethomas and Bassaleg.

There were also developments late in the life of the undertaking in relation to the main route. Red & White had for many years run a Bargoed-Rhymney Bridge service, which shared its route

The fifth Regent V, BWO 585B, was numbered 8. It arrived in 1964 and again had a Massey body. On 27 July 1966 it was seen by Caerphilly Station ready to leave for Newport.

with Gelligaer UDC services 1 and 1A, Ystrad Mynach-Bargoed-Rhymney Bridge, although traditionally each undertaking pretended in its timetables that the other did not exist. At Rhymney Bridge, which was little more than a road junction and interchange point to the north of the town of Rhymney, there were connections with the Merthyr-Rhymney Bridge-Tredegar service also run by Red & White.

One belated consequence of the widespread reorganisation of 1967 was the introduction in August 1968 of new services 149 and 150, which were operated jointly by Bedwas and Machen and Gelligaer UDCs, Western Welsh and Red & White. Caerphilly did not participate as they had had no share in the services being replaced.

The 149 ran Newport-Machen-Bedwas-Caerphilly-Ystrad Mynach-Bargoed-Rhymney Bridge-Tredegar on an hourly headway, and the 150 shared its route as far as Rhymney Bridge and then went to Merthyr. Although that was the basic pattern, in fact it was still necessary to change at Rhymney Bridge on many journeys to Tredegar. Bedwas and Machen indeed ran only as far as

Rhymney Bridge, on three through journeys a day on the very long route and municipal operation right through had to wait until Rhymney Valley DC came into existence. It required a decision of the full Council, rather than the transport committee, for Bedwas to agree this new departure.

It thus came about that in the last six years of the 52 for which the undertaking ran its distinctive vehicles were seen over a much larger area of South Wales than had ever been the case before. In consequence of the new extended services, and in pursuance of its earlier resolution, the Council took delivery in 1968 of its largest vehicle ever, and the first Leyland ever owned.

It was in many ways, however, an anachronism, as it reverted to an exposed radiator, the last such delivered to any operator in South Wales, and was in addition one of the few 30 feet long double-deckers with lowbridge configuration and bench seats upstairs. It achieved some fame as the last vehicle ever built with that unpopular layout, and subsequently passed into preservation, as indeed did two of the AEC Regent V/Massey vehicles and one of the 1951 AEC half cab single-deckers.

The best known vehicle owned by Bedwas & Machen was also its first Leyland. The last lowbridge vehicle built in this country was number 6, PAX 466F, which reverted to an exposed radiator. It is seen here on 4 July 1968, within a few weeks of delivery, in Bargoed.

The only modern development associated with the PD3 was its provision of platform doors, which were desirable on the longer journeys.

The financial position did improve as a result of the new arrangements, and although in early 1969 Caerphilly wanted to discuss the amalgamation of the two undertakings, Bedwas was sufficiently confident by July of that year to rebuff its neighbour yet again, on the basis that it was fiscally stable and in any event more radical changes in local government areas were in the pipeline. The revival in economic fortunes was further demonstrated in the following year, when the Council opposed the company operators raising fares. The number of passengers carried had remained at around the one million mark from 1954 to 1963, and even in 1970, after the extensions described, it was all but 900,000, a very small decline when seen against the national picture.

Between 1968 and 1971 there was, however, a rapid volte face in the undertaking's policy relating to new vehicles, which coincided with the illness and subsequent retirement of EV Coleman in late 1969 and his replacement the following year by the Council's last omnibus manager, Haydn Williams. The move to one person operation was by then becoming irresistible.

In September 1969 it was decided to purchase one single-decker and one double-decker, but then decided to proceed only with the single-decker, the first to be purchased since the Regals in 1951. In fact, the remaining four vehicles which were acquired between 1971 and 1973 were all Leyland Leopard high capacity single-deckers suitable for one man operation, although there were three different makes of bodywork fitted.

The first, 7 (YWO 121J) arrived in May 1971, with bodywork by Northern Counties, who had taken over the business of their Wigan neighbours Massey. The next, 9 (GAX 423L) came in November 1972 but was bodied by Willowbrook and was very similar to four other vehicles purchased by Caerphilly at that time. When the next new vehicles were required, it was thought that Willowbrook's quotation was too high, so the last two buses bought, 10 and 11 (OAX 74/5M) had bodywork by East Lancashire. They did not arrive until December 1973, so ran for only a very few months as Bedwas and Machen vehicles in the historic blue and white livery.

There were a few minor changes to services in the last few years. In May 1973 a new and replacement bus station was opened in Newport, in Kingsway, near the previous Dock Street premises. In 1972 the old Pandy Road route was resurrected for a few months before Christmas, as an experiment, and the following year it was finally decided to run the Graig-y-Rhacca route via the more direct Hillside Terrace, although this does not appear ever to have been implemented during municipal operation.

In April 1974, on the coming into effect of the Local Government Act 1972, the UDC fleet was incorporated into that of the new Rhymney Valley DC, and the Bedwas garage was closed, with all vehicles concentrated either at the former Caerphilly premises in Mill Lane or the former Gelligaer garage in New Road, Tir-y-berth, Hengoed. The newer Bedwas vehicles were taken into the Rhymney Valley fleet and most were repainted. The Graig-y-Rhacca service was developed into a frequent cross-Caerphilly facility, being joined to the Sengenydd service and running every 20 minutes.

In due course Rhymney Valley transformed itself into Inter Valley Link Ltd., over-expanded and, as with other South Wales former municipal operators, found that the new commercial world was somewhat unforgiving. In 1989 operations were taken over by National Welsh (which itself had only a short future ahead of it at that time) and all former Bedwas and Machen vehicles were sold.

Services in the area are now run largely by Stagecoach, and Graig-y-Rhacca has a basic service every 10 minutes, the best ever, via the direct route omitting Bryntirion.

The livery of Bedwas and Machen vehicles remained basically the same throughout the operations of the undertaking. The Council adopted what is usually described as powder blue from the very beginning, although without more this is somewhat misleading to those who did not have the privilege of seeing the vehicles in operation. The use of the term powder in relation to the colour blue arises from the old Chinese practice of blowing powdered cobalt over a surface and it can, in fact, cover a variety of shades. The Bedwas and Machen shade is more properly described as deep powder blue and was not dissimilar to the traditional Pontypridd livery, but very distinctive when seen against most of the stage carriage vehicles in the immediate area: Caerphilly used a deep green, and both Western Welsh and Red & White had predominantly, or in the former case almost entirely, red liveries.

The blue colour, with white relief, was adopted from the very beginning and certainly by the 1930s was fully lined out in gold with the full name of the Council on the waist rail. Over the years the white became somewhat creamier and in due course the insignia of the Council were not applied to the sides of the vehicle as an economy measure. As double-deckers were introduced, there were various detailed changes which are set out in relation to the specific vehicles described. In later years, double-deckers carried large white/cream fleet numbers on each side of the front destination box. Although the insignia were removed, the name of the authority was always displayed prominently and on the underfloor engined single-deckers which were introduced in the last few years it was set out in large letters beneath the windscreen.

Certainly in post 1950 years, the Council was notable for the immaculate presentation of its vehicles. The small size of the undertaking meant that it was possible to achieve such standards, and also that employees took a real pride in preparing the buses for service, although the Council was not immune from sporadic labour problems. It is notorious that blue weathers badly, but this was overcome. Such despoiling features as advertisements were generally avoided, although the two half cab single-deckers which arrived in 1951 were fitted with the large wooden boards on each side for that purpose.

Because of the limited workshop facilities, much of the heavy overhauling, bodywork and painting repairs were carried out at the premises of Caerphilly UDC. The undertaking was also run with appropriate regard to economy: during the evenings and on Sundays the depot was locked up, and there were no emergency staff on duty, but buses were out on the road. Inspections were generally carried out in later years on behalf of Bedwas by Caerphilly UDC staff, and indeed in 1965 the two bodies agreed a fee of £2 per week for that service. The office staff was similarly small in number, and was headed by the efficient chief clerk, Miss M Trott, who held that position from 1946 until the cessation of operations.

The table after the fleet list in the next section shows the size of the fleet over the years, which was generally 3 before the War and 6 or 7 thereafter. There were occasional dips which were caused by vehicles becoming unroadworthy and their replacements being delayed, but gaps were filled by hiring from Caerphilly or elsewhere, as had happened after the 1943 fire.

The reversion to single-deckers began in 1971 with the arrival of number 7, YWO 121J, a Leyland Leopard with Northern Counties body, seen here in Caerphilly on 31 May 1972 followed by one of the Regents.

In 1972 a second Leopard arrived, but this time it had a Willowbrook body and proclaimed its ownership several times over. It was seen here in Caerphilly on 10 September 1973.

Willowbrook-bodied Leyland Leopard of 1972 is shown the new depot in Bedwas in November 1974. It is now in the ownership of Rhymney Valley UDC and has been renumbered 93

The last two vehicles bought by Bedwas were also Leopards, but had East Lancs bodies. They ran for only a few months for the Council, before passing to Rhymney Valley. OAX 74M is shown at Bedwas on 17 November 1974.

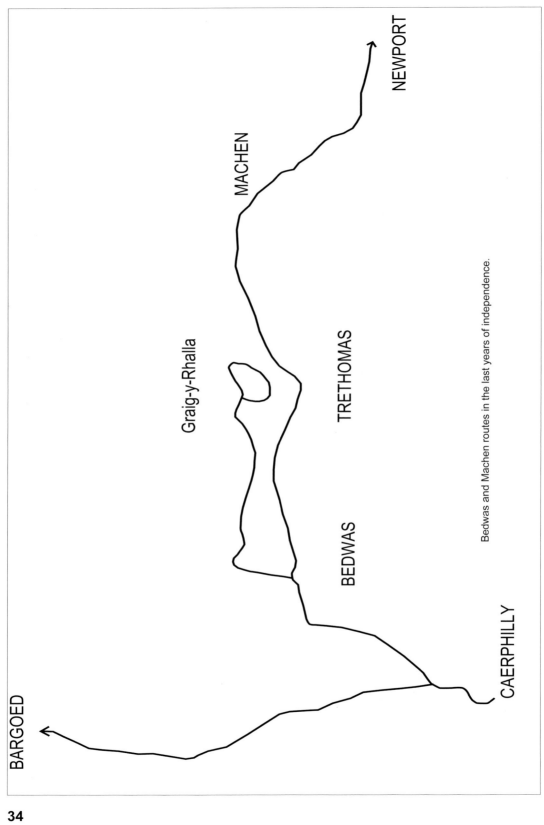

BARGOED

NEWPORT

MACHEN

Graig-y-Rhalla

TRETHOMAS

BEDWAS

CAERPHILLY

Bedwas and Machen routes in the last years of independence.

34

FLEET LIST

Fleet numbers were not allocated or carried until 1951 and so when set out below they refer only to the period after that.

Information is set out below as follows:

FLEET NUMBER	INDEX NUMBER	CHASSIS	BODYWORK

1922

	AX 3860	STRAKER-SQUIRE A		?STRAKER-SQUIRE B32R
	AX 3861	STRAKER-SQUIRE A		?STRAKER-SQUIRE B32R

These vehicles were both placed in service in January 1922 to commence operations and remained with the Council until 1930, a long period for vehicles at the time. They were both repaired by Straker-Squire in June 1924 and reconditioned in 1928. They were sold to Child and Pullen, Ipswich, a dealer, in March 1930, as was the third Straker-Squire, which was new in 1924. Straker-Squire was quite a prominent manufacturer in the post-First World War period, supplying cars and trucks as well as buses. However, it did not survive the death of its founder, Sidney Straker, in a hunting accident in 1926. They had premises in Edmonton but also in Bristol, rather nearer to South Wales.

An offside view of Straker-Squire AX 3861

1923

	AW 5843	KARRIER H	?KARRIER B33F

This vehicle arrived in September 1923. It was one man operated, which was not prohibited at that time: the Road Traffic Act 1930 precluded the running of one man vehicles unless capacity was restricted to 20. It had been ordered as a 28 seater but the capacity was increased. It was withdrawn in July 1926 and sold back to Karriers as dealers.

1924

	AX 6648	STRAKER-SQUIRE A		STRAKER-SQUIRE B32R

This vehicle, another Straker-Squire, was new in November 1924. As with the other two, it was sold to Child and Pullen in March 1930.

1926

	AX 9157	KARRIER KL	?KARRIER B39F

In July 1926 the Council acquired its second Karrier in replacement for the first. In March 1930 it was demoted for use on workers' services only and in late 1931 it was sold to Albion Motors, Scotstoun, acting as dealers. It was later acquired for scrap in December 1933 by Watts (Factors), Lydney, part of the Red & White empire.

1930

	HS 4281	ALBION PJ26	? B25F
	HS 4284	ALBION PJ26	? B25F

These two vehicles were acquired second-hand in January 1930 from Albion Motors, again acting as dealers. They were originally new to Port Glasgow Motor Company, Port Glasgow, in May 1926: it was then and later very unusual for a municipal operator to buy used vehicles. In October 1932 HS4284 was reseated to 20 in order that it might be used for one man operation. The other vehicle, HS4281, was not thought to be worth converting and was sold back to Albion in that month: it later went to a showman and was not withdrawn until 1947. HS4284 was also resold to Albion, but not until October 1935.

	YN 3799	AEC NS	LGOC B30R

Another unusual second-hand vehicle for a municipality, in this case acquired about March 1930 through Child and Pullen, was this ex LGOC AEC, new in April 1926 and formerly numbered NS1738. It had a Daimler engine and was similar to an ADC coach chassis and Bedwas always termed it as a Daimler. It was withdrawn and sold for scrap in 1933.

	TY 3841	GILFORD LL15	? B26F

The fourth second-hand vehicle acquired in 1930 was this Gilford, new in October 1927 to Robert Emmerson & Co. Ltd., Throckley, Northumberland, which then passed with that company's business to United Automobile in January 1930: they sold it on very quickly, in about April 1930 to Bedwas. It was withdrawn and then scrapped in 1935.

1932

	WO 6266	ALBION PW65	PARK ROYAL B32R

In 1932 the Council was able again to purchase a brand new vehicle, the first since 1926: this was a reflection of the very harsh economic climate at the time. The new vehicle appeared in May 1932 and heralded a new era of Albion dominance of the small fleet. This was one of the vehicles destroyed in the depot fire in February 1943.

Pictures of pre-war vehicles owned by the Council are few and far between and, of course, the fleet was completely destroyed in the depot fire of 1943. One vehicle which was burned out was Albion/Park Royal WO 36266 of 1932.

1933

	WO 6969	ALBION PW65	PARK ROYAL B32R

In March 1933 a second new Albion arrived. It too was burned out in the depot fire, although at the time the engine had been removed elsewhere for overhaul, and it was later advertised for sale separately. It was also proposed at about this time to buy further Albions from Griffin of Brynmawr, part of the Red & White group, but this did not progress.

1936

	AAX 785	ALBION PW69	? B32R

The third vehicle destroyed in the depot fire in 1943 was also an Albion, which had been acquired in March 1936.

1943

	EWO 406	BEDFORD OWB	DUPLE B32F
3	EWO 544	BEDFORD OWB	DUPLE B32F
	EWO 574	BEDFORD OWB	DUPLE B32F

These three small Bedfords were, of course, allocated under wartime conditions; there can scarcely have been an operator which required new vehicles more than Bedwas, which had been forced to borrow from its neighbours Caerphilly to keep its service running. They arrived in March, May and July 1944 respectively and the first two were later reseated to B28F. Their stay in the fleet was relatively short, though, because of the increase in traffic. In November 1950 the first and third vehicles were sold to Morlais Services Ltd. of Merthyr. The one remainimg, EWO 544, survived long enough to receive a fleet number and had its chassis reconditioned in April 1950 and its body similarly treated in February 1951. It was sold in 1954 and converted to a pantechnicon.

Bedford OWB EWO 544, later numbered 3, is seen in Caerphilly on the Pandy Road service.

1944

	EWO 924	BEDFORD OWB	DUPLE B32F

The fourth and last new OWB arrived in May 1944 and was sold with the other two to Morlais in November 1950.

Bedwas' first double-deckers were due to be the two Leyland TD1s from Wigan, but in fact they arrived after the two Albions. On Roy Marshall's trip to the area on 16 July 1949, he caught the second of the pair of Leylands, EK 7913, in Caerphilly about to leave for Trethomas.

1947

1	EK 7912	LEYLAND TD1	LEYLAND L24/24R
	EK 7913	LEYLAND TD1	LEYLAND L24/24R

These two double-deckers in the fleet were purchased new by Wigan Corporation in December 1930, so were of considerable antiquity when acquired by Bedwas. Wigan had a considerable reputation for looking after its vehicles and had fitted these with diesel engines. They were withdrawn in 1946 and passed to Watts (Factors) of Lydney in 1947, who then overhauled them. They were then painted by Welsh Metal Industries Ltd. of Caerphilly and entered service in October 1949 and September 1948 respectively. They were only a short term answer to the need for new vehicles: EK 7913 needed a

In 1947 Bedwas purchased a fifth Bedford OWB, second-hand from Ralphs of Abertillery. It lasted longer than any of the others and was not withdrawn until 1956. It was again photographed by Roy Marshall in 1949, in Machen.

new engine in July 1950 but was almost immediately withdrawn after it was found that the body too needed attention and it was sold to Morlais, Merthyr, for spares. EK 7912 was rebuilt in 1949 prior to entering service, but lasted only until October 1951 when it was withdrawn and sold to a showman.

2	EWO 380	BEDFORD OWB	DUPLE B32F

The fifth OWB owned by the Council was new in January 1943 to Ralphs Services Ltd., Abertillery, which was associated with Red & White. It was acquired via Arlingtons, dealers, in November 1947 and later had both chassis and body overhauled. It was then reseated to B28F and remained in the fleet until June 1956, well after all the other Bedfords. It was used to institute the Pandy Road service.

1948

4	GWO 482	ALBION CX19	WELSH METAL INDUSTRIES L31/26R
5	HAX 340	ALBION CX19	WELSH METAL INDUSTRIES L31/26R

The Council's first new double-deckers arrived in 1948. They were an unusual purchase and may well have been partly dictated by the availability of vehicles at a time of enormous demand, and also by the desire to support local industry if possible. The Albion CX19 chassis was relatively rare, particularly outside Scotland, but was purchased by the Red & White group. Welsh Metal Industries was one of the many small firms which attempted to take advantage of the need for bus bodies and indeed the engineer of the Council is said to have been involved in their design. They were quite different in outline, with GWO 482, which arrived in February 1948 having a very angular design and its fellow, which arrived in October that year, having a more rounded profile. However, both were all-aluminium and both originally had putty mounted windows, a particular speciality of WMI, which caused the glass to rattle as the vehicle went along the road. Neither body was satisfactory in service. Number 4 was repaired by WMI in October 1948 and again in April 1951 and then rebuilt with conventional rubber-mounted windows by Romilly Motors of Cardiff in October 1952. It was withdrawn in 1959 and then ran for Contract Bus Services of Caerwent. Number 5 was rebuilt with rubber mounted windows by Caerphilly UDC in June 1954 and was withdrawn in 1961 and also sold to Contract Bus Services.

GWO 482 is seen here in May 1956 in Caerphilly, by which time the radiator had also been replaced.

6	JWO 354	AEC REGAL III	BRUCE B35R
7	JWO3 55	AEC REGAL III	BRUCE B35R

After the experience with WMI, Bedwas and Machen turned to another local coachbuilder, Bruce of Cardiff, for its next two bodies, which were mounted on AEC Regal III chassis and arrived in January and February 1951 respectively. They came just as half cabs and rear entrances on single-deckers were beginning to disappear as the new fashion for underfloor engines and front entrances swept all

Welsh Metal Industries-bodied Albion HAX 340 in its rebuilt state.

The later livery applied to theAEC Regals included white around the windows. JWO 354 was at Caerphilly on 8 June 1966 on the Llanfabon service, without advertising boards.

before it. However, unlike the Albion double-deckers, the bodies, which were constructed on East Lancs frames as was much of Bruce's output, were handsome and lasted well. The unusual feature of these vehicles was the large wooden advertisement boards which were fitted on each side. They were delivered with only a band of white around the waist rail to relieve the blue, but later the windows and surrounds were thus painted. They lasted until May 1967 (6, which went for scrap) and July 1971 in the case of 7, which went for preservation, returned for the last day of operation by the Council, and later was exported to South Africa for transport in a game park.

8	KWO 216	AEC REGENT III	NORTHERN COUNTIES H30/26R

The only highbridge double-decker ever owned by the UDC was this fine AEC Regent, which was built with a batch of 3 similar vehicles for Aberdare UDC, which comprehensively renewed its fleet at this time. However, unlike Aberdare, Bedwas did not specify wooden slatted seats for its vehicles. It was bought through the AEC agents, Romilly Motors of Cardiff: the demand for new vehicles had

The only highbridge double-decker ever owned by the Council was AEC Regent III KWO 216, numbered 8, built with a series for Aberdare with handsome Northern Counties bodywork.

slowed down by this time. The vehicle arrived in May 1952 and was retained until September 1964 and later ran for RI Davies of Merthyr. South Wales has many low bridges, and although there were none on the stage routes run by Bedwas, a highbridge vehicle was undoubtedly restricted in the area. It had received cream window surrounds by 1960 and flashing trafficators by 1963.

1956

9	PWO 783	AEC REGENT V	LONGWELL GREEN L27/28R

The Council was pleased with its AEC vehicles and returned to that manufacturer for its next vehicle, which again had some unusual features. It was an exposed radiator Regent V, which was somewhat dated by this time, with bodywork by Longwell Green, a small company situated outside Bristol which provided vehicles for a number of municipalities in South Wales at this time. The vehicle was reseated to 29/28 very shortly after delivery and later to 31/28 by 1962, reflecting the increasing traffic handled. It arrived in November 1956 and was withdrawn after a relatively short life in September 1968 and sold for scrap. It was the last vehicle in the banded blue and white livery, later replaced by having white around the windows by about 1959, and was also the last vehicle with the municipal crest on its side.

1957

10	RAX 583	AEC REGENT V	MASSEY L29/28R

By 1957 the Council had established a clear preference for AEC chassis: this vehicle, unlike its predecessor, had a more usual "new look" enclosed radiator. It was delivered in April 1957 with a new livery with greater use of cream but only on the lower deck but was later repainted with cream window surrounds on both decks. It was withdrawn in December 1973 and sold in early 1974 to Gelligaer UDC, from where it passed to Rhymney Valley DC in April 1974 as number 83: it was withdrawn the following year after never being repainted into the new authority's livery.

On 11 May 1966 PWO 783 the AEC Regent V with Longwell Green body was seen in Caerphilly en route for Trethomas.

The Trethomas service was extended to Graig-y-Rhacca and Massey-bodied AEV Regent V number 10 was seen on 30 June 1969 in Caerphilly on that service.

1959

11	UWO 498	AEC REGENT V	MASSEY L31/28R

The 1959 delivery continued where that in 1957 had left off. Massey Brothers in Wigan was a small enough bodybuilder to be concerned with single-vehicle orders and was particularly involved with municipalities. This vehicle arrived in June 1959 and was later repainted with cream window surrounds on both decks. It was loaned to Gelligaer for a time in early 1974, but then passed to Rhymney Valley as 98 in April 1974: it was used as a training vehicle until being dismantled for spares in about 1976.

On 4 June 1969, the second Massey-bodied Regent number 11 was caught in Caerphilly, well laden on the busy Graig-y-Rhacca service.

1961

5	422 CAX	AEC REGENT V	MASSEY L31/28R

The third successive Massey bodied Regent V to join the fleet arrived in December 1961 and was again later repainted with cream surrounds to all the windows. It was transferred to Rhymney Valley in April 1974 as 91 and later renumbered 82. It never received a new livery and was used as a training vehicle from 1975 to 1980 when it was withdrawn and sold for preservation.

422 CAX was later repainted with white surrounds to the upper windows. On 30 June 1969 it was in Caerphilly.

1964

8	BWO 585B	AEC REGENT V	MASSEY L31/28R

The last AEC Regent V purchased arrived in September 1964, was again repainted into the ultimate livery, and again passed to Rhymney Valley in 1974, in its case as 92. It was disposed of in late 1979 and purchased for preservation.

Number 8 is seen here in Caerphilly on 8 September 1973, not long before the end of operations. It is running on the long Newport-Rhymney Bridge service in Caerphilly.

1968

6	PAX 466F	LEYLAND PD3/4	MASSEY L35/33RD

There can be very few municipal operators which until 1968 had never operated a Leyland. This was a somewhat anachronistic vehicle by the time it was delivered: it has become well-known as the last vehicle built in this country of traditional lowbridge layout and one of the few such constructed on a 30 foot long chassis. It also reverted to an exposed radiator at a time when they had become very rare. Platform doors were provided for the first time, as by 1968 the UDC was participating in the longer journeys to Bargoed and then beyond. It arrived in June 1968, passed to Rhymney Valley in 1974, but was repainted in traditional Bedwas colours to celebrate the sixtieth anniversary of the commencement of services in 1982. It was then sold to Stevensons of Uttoxeter and then in 1994 for preservation, as befits its historical significance.

On 4 June 1969 the final lowbridge double-decker built was seen in Caerphilly bound for Newport.

1971

7	YWO 121J	LEYLAND PSU3B/2R	NORTHERN COUNTIES B53F

There was a complete change of policy after the delivery of the Leyland PD3: one man operation by larger capacity single-deckers was the order of the day and in May 1971 this Leyland Leopard arrived. Massey had ceased body building and had been taken over by their neighbours. It was transferred to RVDC as 97 in 1974 and sold on in September 1984, eventually being used for internal transport by British Steel at Redcar.

On 31 May 1972, Leyland Leopard number 7 was seen at Caerphilly Station terminus ready to leave for Newport.

1972

9	GAX 423L	LEYLAND PSU3B/2R	WILLOWBROOK B53F

Another Leyland Leopard followed in November 1972 but this time it had bodywork by Willowbrook, a new departure, and one which followed the example of Caerphilly, which took five similar buses that year. It was transferred to RVDC in 1974 as 93 and as an almost new vehicle survived to be transferred to Inter Valley Link Ltd., the successors to the local authority operation, in October 1986. It was withdrawn in 1989 on the takeover of that company by National Welsh, and sold for service in Scotland but soon scrapped.

The second Leopard with East Lancs bodywork, number 11, passed to Rhymney Valley District Council but was not repainted for some time. On 17 November 1974 it was still in Bedwas livery.

| 10 | OAX 74M | LEYLAND PSU3B/2R | EAST LANCS B51F |
| 11 | OAX 75M | LEYLAND PSU3B/2R | EAST LANCS B51F |

The Council's final two vehicles were also Leopards, but they carried the third make of bodywork on the four modern single-deckers. East Lancs supplied these, which arrived as late as December 1973 so only ran in Bedwas colours for a very short time. They too passed to RVDC as 94 and 95 respectively and then in 1986 to Inter Valley. In 1989 they were sold on the takeover and saw some further service.

East Lancs-bodied Leyland Leopard number 10, at Tiryberth near the former Gelligaer garage, on 16 April 1974, just after the transfer.

FLEET SIZE YEAR BY YEAR

This table shows the size of the fleet at the end of each calendar year in which there was a material change, with subdivision into single- and double-deckers.

YEAR	S/D	D/D	TOTAL
1922	2		2
1923	3		3
1924	4		4
1930	5		5
1931	4		4
1934	3		3
1935	2		2
1936	3		3
1944	4		4
1947	5	2	7
1948	5	4	9
1950	2	3	5
1951	4	3	7
1954	3	3	6
1956	2	4	6
1957	2	5	7
1967	1	5	6
1972	2	5	7
1973	4	5	9

BEDWAS AND MACHEN URBAN DISTRICT COUNCIL OMNIBUS SERVICE

MONDAY TO SATURDAY.

	a.m.	a.m.	a.m.	a.m.	a.m.	a.m.	a.m.	a.m.	a.m.	p.m.	p.m.	p.m.	p.m.	p.m.	p.m.	p.m.	p.m.	p.m.	p.m.	p.m.	p.m.	p.m.
Machen ..	5 45	..	6 30	7 40	8 50	9 30	10 05	11 05	12 05	1 05	2 05	3 05	4 05	5 05	6 05	7 05	8 05	9 05	10 05	11 05	11 30	
Trethomas ..	5 50	..	6 40	7 50	9 00	9 40	10 10	11 10	12 10	1 10	2 10	3 10	4 10	5 10	6 10	7 10	8 10	9 10	10 10	11 10	11 40	
Bedwas Garage ..	..	..	6 45	7 55	9 05	9 45	10 15	11 15	12 15	1 15	2 15	3 15	4 15	5 15	6 15	7 15	8 15	9 15	10 15	11 15	11 45	
Caerphilly ..	..	..	6 50	8 00	9 10	9 50	10 25	11 25	12 25	1 25	2 25	3 25	4 25	5 25	6 25	7 25	8 25	9 25	10 25	11 25	..	

	a.m.	a.m.	a.m.	a.m.	a.m.	a.m.	p.m.	p.m.	p.m.	p.m.	p.m.	p.m.	p.m.	p.m.	p.m.	p.m.	p.m.	p.m.	p.m.
Caerphilly ..	5 30	..	6 55	8 10	9 10	10 05	11 05	12 05	1 05	2 05	3 05	4 05	5 05	6 05	7 05	8 05	9 05	10 05	11 05
Bedwas Garage ..	5 35	..	7 00	8 15	9 15	10 10	11 10	12 10	1 10	2 10	3 10	4 10	5 10	6 10	7 10	8 10	9 10	10 10	11 10
Trethomas ..	5 35	..	7 05	8 20	9 20	10 15	11 15	12 15	1 15	2 15	3 15	4 15	5 15	6 15	7 15	8 15	9 15	10 15	11 15
Machen ..	5 45	..	7 15	8 30	9 30	10 25	11 25	12 25	1 25	2 25	3 25	4 25	5 25	6 25	7 25	8 25	9 25	10 25	11 25

SATURDAY SERVICE (Additional)

	a.m.	a.m.	a.m.	a.m.	p.m.	p.m.	p.m.	p.m.	p.m.	p.m.	p.m.	p.m.	p.m.	p.m.
Machen ..	10 50	11 20	12 10	12 50	1 20	2 00	2 35	3 15	4 15	5 15	6 15	7 15	8 15	9 15
Trethomas ..	10 55	11 25	12 15	12 55	1 25	2 05	2 40	3 20	4 20	5 20	6 20	7 20	8 20	9 20
Bedwas Garage ..	11 00	11 30	12 20	1 00	1 30	2 10	2 45	3 25	4 25	5 25	6 25	7 25	8 25	9 25
Caerphilly ..	11 10	11 40	12 30	1 10	1 40	2 20	2 55	3 35	4 35	5 35	6 35	7 35	8 35	9 35

	a.m.	a.m.	a.m.	p.m.	p.m.	p.m.	p.m.	p.m.	p.m.	p.m.	p.m.	p.m.	p.m.
Caerphilly ..	11 00	11 35	12 25	1 10	1 35	2 15	2 50	3 50	4 50	5 50	6 50	7 50	8 50
Bedwas Garage ..	11 05	11 40	12 30	1 15	1 40	2 20	2 55	3 55	4 55	5 55	6 55	7 55	8 55
Trethomas ..	11 15	..	12 35	1 20	1 45	2 30	3 00	4 00	5 00	6 00	7 00	8 00	9 00
Machen ..	11 50	..	..	..	..	2 40	3 10	4 10	5 10	6 10	7 10	8 10	9 10

SUNDAY SERVICE

	a.m.	a.m.	a.m.	p.m.	p.m.	p.m.	p.m.	p.m.	p.m.	p.m.	p.m.	p.m.	p.m.	p.m.	p.m.	p.m.	p.m.	p.m.
Machen ..	..	..	..	12 45	1 20	2 00	2 30	3 00	3 30	4 30	5 30	6 30	7 30	8 30	9 30	10 30	11 05	
Trethomas ..	..	..	..	12 50	1 30	2 45	3 15	3 45	4 45	5 45	6 45	7 45	8 45	9 45	10 40	11 25		
Bedwas Garage ..	10 50	11 20	12 10	12 55	1 40	2 50	3 30	4 00	5 00	6 00	7 00	8 00	9 00	10 00	10 50	11 30		
Caerphilly ..	11 00	11 30	12 20	1 00	1 45	3 10	3 35	4 10	5 10	6 10	7 10	8 10	9 10	10 10	11 10	..		

	a.m.	a.m.	p.m.	p.m.	p.m.	p.m.	p.m.	p.m.	p.m.	p.m.	p.m.	p.m.	p.m.	p.m.	p.m.
Caerphilly ..	11 00	12 40	1 00	2 15	3 05	4 05	5 05	6 05	7 05	8 05	9 05	10 05	11 05		
Bedwas Garage ..	11 05	12 45	1 05	2 20	3 15	4 15	5 15	6 15	7 15	8 15	9 15	10 15	11 15		
Trethomas ..	11 15	..	1 10	2 30	3 25	4 25	5 25	6 25	7 25	8 25	9 25	10 25	11 15		
Machen ..	11 50	..	1 20	2 40	3 10	4 10	5 10	6 10	7 10	8 10	9 10	10 10	—		

PANDY ROAD.

	a.m.	a.m.	a.m.	a.m.	p.m. S.O.	p.m. S.O.	p.m.	p.m.	p.m.	p.m.	p.m.	p.m.	p.m.	p.m. S.O.	p.m. S.O.
Caerphilly ..	8 00	9 00	11 00	12 40	1 00	2 00	3 00	4 00	5 00	6 00	7 00	8 40	9 40	9 00	10 00
Pandy Road ..	8 10	9 10	11 10	12 50	1 10	2 10	3 10	4 10	5 10	6 10	7 10	8 50	9 50	9 10	10 10

	a.m.	a.m.	a.m.	a.m.	p.m.	p.m.	p.m.	p.m.	p.m.	p.m.	p.m.	p.m. S.O.	p.m. S.O.
Pandy Road ..	8 15	9 10	11 15	1 15	2 15	3 15	4 15	5 15	6 45	7 45	8 15	9 15	
Caerphilly ..	8 25	9 20	11 25	1 25	2 25	3 25	4 25	5 25	7 00	7 25	8 25	9 25	

NO SUNDAY SERVICE

BRYNFEDW.

	a.m.	a.m. S.O.	p.m.	p.m.	p.m.	p.m.	p.m.	p.m.	p.m.	p.m. S.E.	p.m.
Caerphilly ..	11 40	12 50	2 40	3 40	6 20	7 20	9 20	10 20	7 40	9 40	
Brynfedw ..	11 50	12 50	2 50	3 50	6 30	7 30	9 30	10 30	7 50	9 50	

	a.m. S.O.	p.m.	p.m.	p.m.	p.m.	p.m.	p.m.	p.m.	p.m.
Brynfedw ..	11 50	12 50	2 50	3 30	6 30	7 30	9 30	8 50	9 50
Caerphilly ..	12 00	1 00	3 00	4 00	6 40	7 40	9 40	9 00	10 00

NO SUNDAY SERVICE.

STANDARD STREET.

WEEKDAYS

	a.m.	a.m.	p.m.	p.m.	p.m.	p.m.	p.m.	p.m.
Caerphilly ..	9 20	10 20	1 20	4 20	5 20	6 20	7 20	8 20
Standard Street ..	9 30	10 30	1 30	4 30	5 30	6 30	7 30	8 30

	a.m.	a.m.	p.m.	p.m.	p.m.	p.m.
Standard Street ..	9 30	10 30	5 30	6 30	7 30	8 30
Caerphilly ..	9 40	10 40	5 40	6 40	7 40	8 40

SATURDAYS

	a.m.	a.m.	p.m.	p.m.	p.m.	p.m.	p.m.	p.m.	p.m.
Caerphilly ..	9 20	10 20	1 20	3 20	4 20	5 20	6 20	7 20	8 20
Standard St. ..	9 30	10 30	1 30	3 30	4 30	5 30	6 30	7 30	8 30

	a.m.	a.m.	p.m.	p.m.	p.m.	p.m.	p.m.	p.m.
Standard St. ..	9 30	10 40	1 50	3 50	4 50	5 50	6 50	7 50
Caerphilly ..	9 40	10 40	2 00	4 00	5 00			

SUNDAYS

	p.m.	p.m.	p.m.	p.m.
Caerphilly ..	..	6 20	7 20	8 20
Standard Street ..	..	6 30	7 30	8 30

	p.m.	p.m.	p.m.	p.m.
Standard Street ..	5 30	6 30	7 30	8 30
Caerphilly ..	5 40	6 40	7 40	8 40

S.E.—Denotes Saturdays excepted.
S.O.—Denotes Saturdays Only.

FOR CONDITIONS UNDER WHICH PASSENGERS ARE CARRIED SEE RULES PUBLISHED UNDER COUNCIL'S BYE-LAWS